# IT'S TIME TO EAT COLLARD GREENS

# It's Time to Eat COLLARD GREENS

## Walter the Educator

Silent King Books
A WhichHead Entertainment Imprint

Copyright © 2024 by Walter the Educator

All rights reserved. No part of this book may be reproduced in any manner whatsoever without written per- mission except in the case of brief quotations embodied in critical articles and reviews.

First Printing, 2024

Disclaimer

This book is a literary work; the story is not about specific persons, locations, situations, and/or circumstances unless mentioned in a historical context. Any resemblance to real persons, locations, situations, and/or circumstances is coincidental. This book is for entertainment and informational purposes only. The author and publisher offer this information without warranties expressed or implied. No matter the grounds, neither the author nor the publisher will be accountable for any losses, injuries, or other damages caused by the reader's use of this book. The use of this book acknowledges an understanding and acceptance of this disclaimer.

It's Time to Eat COLLARD GREENS is a collectible early learning book by Walter the Educator suitable for all ages belonging to Walter the Educator's Time to Eat Book Series. Collect more books at WaltertheEducator.com

**USE THE EXTRA SPACE TO TAKE NOTES AND DOCUMENT YOUR MEMORIES**

# COLLARD GREENS

It's time to eat, come take a seat,

## It's Time to Eat

# Collard Greens

Collard greens are a tasty treat!

Big and leafy, green and bright,

They'll make your tummy feel just right.

Collard greens grow tall and wide,

In the garden, side by side.

Their leaves are strong, they're full of power,

To help you run and play for hours.

Cook them up with a little steam,

Or stir them into a yummy dream.

Add a pinch of spice, a little zest,

Collard greens are simply the best!

You can chop them small or leave them whole,

They're a veggie that's good for your soul.

Full of vitamins, they help you grow,

Collard greens give you a healthy glow.

# It's Time to Eat

# Collard Greens

Imagine they're capes for a veggie king,

Or sails on a boat that the wind can swing.

But on your plate, they're ready to munch,

A leafy green treat for lunch or brunch!

Crunch, crunch, crunch with every chew,

Collard greens are good for you!

They help you jump, they help you run,

They're a superfood full of fun!

Serve them with cornbread or rice so nice,

Or maybe a soup with beans and spice.

Collard greens love to share their taste,

No part of them will go to waste!

Some like them fresh, others like them slow,

Cooked in a pot where flavors grow.

No matter the way, they'll make you grin,

# It's Time to Eat

# Collard Greens

Collard greens are a win-win-win!

Take your fork and take a bite,

Feel the goodness, light and bright.

Collard greens are here to stay,

To make you strong every day!

Thank you, greens, for all you do,

For being healthy, tasty too.

We love collard greens, leafy and fine,

# It's Time to Eat Collard Greens

A vegetable treat that's simply divine!

# ABOUT THE CREATOR

Walter the Educator is one of the pseudonyms for Walter Anderson. Formally educated in Chemistry, Business, and Education, he is an educator, an author, a diverse entrepreneur, and he is the son of a disabled war veteran.
"Walter the Educator" shares his time between educating and creating. He holds interests and owns several creative projects that entertain, enlighten, enhance, and educate, hoping to inspire and motivate you. Follow, find new works, and stay up to date with Walter the Educator™ at WaltertheEducator.com

www.ingramcontent.com/pod-product-compliance
Lightning Source LLC
LaVergne TN
LVHW052011060526
838201LV00059B/3972